Freedom From Bondage
Through Scriptural Prayers

From Never Feeling Hunger To Abundance

Priscilla Coleman

Freedom From Bondage Through Scriptural Prayers: From Never Feeling Hunger To Abundance- Priscilla Coleman

All scripture quotations are from the King James Version of the Holy Bible-Brackets are used to display italics words

Copyright ©2015 by Priscilla Coleman

ISBN-13: 978-1519459046
ISBN-10: 1519459041

Printed by CreateSpace, An Amazon.com Company
Kindle Version Available

All rights reserved under International Copyright Law. No part of this book may be reproduced, stored in a retrieval system, or transmitted in any form by any means, electronic, mechanical, photocopying, recording, or otherwise without written permission of the copyright owner the author.

Printed in the United States of America

To Jesus my Lord

"For no man ever yet hated his own flesh; but nourisheth and cherisheth it, even as the Lord the church: for we are members of his body, of his flesh, and of his bones."
Ephesians 5:29-30

"...Hearken diligently unto me, and eat ye [that which is] good, and let your soul delight itself in fatness (abundance)."
Isaiah 55:2

Table of Contents

Acknowledgements 7

Introduction 9

God's Will 13

Instructions 15

The Heart of the Matter 19

Faith 23

Have a Good Laugh 27

Steps to Get There 31

Nourish the Whole Being 35

Expectation of Good 39

Don't Give Up! 41

Scriptures

- Morning 43
- Praise 45
- Choose to Eat 47
- Variety of Foods 49
- Meal Time 51
- Healthy Eating 53

- Joy in Eating 55

Salvation Scriptures 57

Acknowledgements

Thanks to my siblings: Joseph Jr., Esther, and Spencer, for support and encouragement

LOVE ALWAYS!

Introduction

"And also that every man should eat and drink, and enjoy the good of all his labour, it [is] the gift of God."
Ecclesiastes 3:13

The purpose of this book is to share what I learned through revelation knowledge of the Word of God to overcome an eating disorder. The National Eating Disorder Association (NEDA), www.nationaleatingdisorders.org, describes what I endured as a None Specific Eating Disorder. In my book "An Overcomers' Journey From the Effects of Abuse Through Scriptural Prayers", I introduce this topic. Nearly fifty years of abuse had an effect on my mental and physical health. One of the effects of abuse was that I never felt hunger, and had no desire to eat.

I enquired of God for the root cause of the eating disorder. The Holy Spirit revealed that I had a sin conscious mentality. As I understand it, this as a mentality of being "wrong" or the answer is "no" to everything where I am concerned. Feelings of guilt and unworthiness also produced restrictions in every area of my life. I discuss freedom from sin consciousness in the before mentioned book.

This is a book of my journey, and Bible verses used to create scriptural prayers. I add my name to make the prayers personal. Blank pages in this book are provided for the reader to create their own scriptural prayers. Lord willing this book shall bring revelation, light and healing in this area to many others.

All scriptural prayers are to be read out loud to aid in the development of faith. The Bible says "Faith [cometh] by hearing, and hearing by the word of God..." **Romans 10:17**

"Then he said unto them (Priscilla), Go your way, eat the fat, and drink the sweet... for [this] day [is] holy unto our Lord: neither be ye sorry; for the joy of the LORD is your strength."
Nehemiah 8:10

God's Will

When I began the journey of learning to overcome the eating disorder I was not aware that there are hundreds of scriptures on the subject of eating and enjoying food in the Bible! "Faith begins when the will of God is known." (Kenneth Copland, www.kcm.org). The process of renewing my mind with the Word of God was essential to receive healing from the eating disorder (**Ephesians 4:23**).

"And ye shall eat in plenty, and be satisfied, and praise the name of the LORD your God, that hath dealt wondrously with you…"
Joel 2:26

"…The living God, who giveth us richly all things to enjoy."
I Timothy 6:17

"Who satisfieth thy mouth with good [things] [so that] thy youth is renewed…"
Psalm 103:5

"And there ye shall eat before the LORD your God, and ye shall rejoice…"
Deuteronomy 12:7

"Then I commended mirth, because a man hath no better thing under the sun, then to eat, and drink and to be merry…which God giveth him under the sun."
Ecclesiastes 8:15

Instructions

I sought God's wisdom and He provided specific instructions to begin my journey. I was prompted to:

- Pray scripture over my meals
- Eat breakfast by 8:00 a.m. everyday
- Take a multivitamin (50+ for women)
- Drink water upon rising
- Eat every two hours
- Eat at least one hot meal everyday
- Exercise three times a week

It took time to successfully obey the instruction to take a multivitamin. I was fearful because if I could not make myself eat, the vitamin would upset my stomach. God could not over ride my fear. But when I made the decision to not be afraid then He helped me.

The Bible says, "There is no fear in love and perfect love casts out fear" (**I John 4:18**). To root out fear, I mediated and confessed out loud the scriptures "I am the disciple Jesus loves" (**John 21:20**) and "I am God's beloved" (**III John 1:2**).

"If any of you lack wisdom, let him ask of God, that giveth to all [men] liberally, and upbraideth not; and it shall be given him. But let him ask in faith, nothing wavering. For he that wavereth is like a wave of the sea driven with the wind and tossed. For let not that man think that he shall receive any thing of

the Lord. A doubled minded man [is] unstable in all his ways."
                    James 1:5-8

"Have not I commanded thee? Be strong and of a good courage; be not afraid...for the LORD thy God [is] with thee..."
                    Joshua 1:9

The Heart of the Matter

The Holy Spirit revealed to successfully eat everyday I needed a desire to eat. The definition of desire according to the Oxford American Dictionary is "a strong feeling of wanting to have something or wish for something to happen." My endeavor to create a desire to eat by reading cookbooks and watching cooking shows on television was helpful only short term.

"Ask God to give you the desires of His heart in a situation and it will become your desire **(Philippians 4:13)**." "A person can not rise above what they think in their heart." (Bill Winston, www.BillWinston.org)

"Delight thyself also in the LORD; and he shall give thee the desires of thine heart. Commit thy way unto the LORD; trust also in him; and he shall bring [it] to pass."
Psalm 34:4-5

"For as he thinketh in his heart, [so is] he…"
Proverbs 23:7

"Keep thy heart with all diligence; for out of it [are] the issues of life."
Proverbs 4:23

I prayed: Heavenly Father in the Name of Jesus, I want to have all the benefits Jesus died, and was raised from the dead to provide for me. I am asking You to give me a desire to eat and teach me how to do it. You created this body and know what it needs for nourishment. Help me to not be a hearer only but a doer of the word **(James 1:22)**. In Jesus' Name, and Lord I praise you. Amen.

"...I (Jesus) am come that they might have life, and that they might have it more abundantly."
John 10:10

"For we are his workmanship, created in Christ Jesus unto good works, which God hath before ordained that we should walk in them."

I mediated, spoke scriptures and put a picture of myself when I was at a healthy weight on my wall. An inside image of myself as healthy, whole and eating a variety of foods is required for it to manifest on the outside. Looking at my body and judging the situation by what is seen will not change the circumstances. As checking the body for symptoms does not produce healing. But believing that "Jesus bore my sickness, and I am healed" **(Isaiah 53:4-5)** produce health.
 "Words are spiritual and create an image in the mind. Speak and think God's words."
(Creflo Dollar, www.creflodollarministries.org)
As I believe, read, speak and mediate the Word of God, transformation occurs in the physical realm.

"While we look not at the things which are seen, but at the things which are not seen: for

the things which are seen [are] temporal; but the things which are not seen [are] eternal."
II Corinthians 4:18

Speaking the Word of God before the problem resolves is how it comes into manifestation. "Action, in belief, brings manifestation in the earth." (Kenneth Copland).

"...And calleth those things which be not as though they were."
Romans 4:17

"We having the same spirit of faith...I believed, and therefore have I spoken..."
II Corinthians 4:13

"But the righteousness which is of faith speaketh..."
Romans 10:6

"Being confident of this very thing, that he which hath begun a good work in you will perform [it] until the day of Jesus Christ."
Philippians 1:6

Faith

It is necessary to keep the door shut on fear in order to keep your faith working. "Fear activates Satan and causes bad things to happen (**I Peter 5:8**). Faith activates God and causes good things to happen (**Hebrews 11:33-34**). When we start wondering why the manifestation of what we have been standing in faith for is not happening, then we are out of faith. Wondering is wavering." (Gloria Copland, www.kcm.org). "What we want is our faith to work so we can receive the grace and favor of God in the situation." (Jerry Savelle, www.jerrysavelle.org).

"Therefore [it is] of faith, that [it might be] by grace…"
Ephesians 4:16

"And being not weak in faith, he (Abraham) considered not his own body now dead…He staggered (wavered) not at the promise of God through unbelief; but was strong in faith, giving glory to God; and being fully persuaded that, what he had promised, he was able also to perform."
Ephesians 4:19-21

"When we have faith, we give God access into our lives. Faith is the channel into the grace of God. And everything we will ever need is in the grace of God. Why does God need access? He gave mankind authority in the earth (**Genesis 1:26**).

Faith pleases God because it gives Him access to do everything He wants to do in our lives."
(Keith Butler, www.keithbutler.org).

"But without faith [it is] impossible to please [him]: for he that cometh to God must believe that he is, and [that] he is a rewarder of them that diligently seek him."
Hebrews 11:6

"For whatsoever is born of God overcometh the world: and this is the victory that overcometh the world [even] our faith."
I John 5:4

Have a Good Laugh

Eating in sorrow and mourning is not good (**Deuteronomy 26:14**). It surprised me that the Bible covers this topic. God cares about every aspect of life (**I Peter 5:7**). Jesus took my sorrow (**Isaiah 53:3**) so I can have joy! Hallelujah!

Joy is different from happiness. Happiness is based on feelings or circumstances. Joy is based on what I know and believe. One of the ways to express joy is to have a good laugh through focusing on scriptures that describe victory in Jesus (**I John 5:4-5**). When I meditate these scriptures, I laugh and laugh until I have a good belly laugh!

"...I'd rather laugh at trouble than align myself with it...I've learned that in order to keep that joy, I must major on the promise and not the problem. Jesus has already overcome, and He's given all authority and power to me. Realizing and believing that is key to not losing any of that precious joy." (Jesse Duplantis, www.jdm.org).

"(Jesus said)...That your joy might be full."
John 15:11

"...The joy of the Lord is my strength."
Nehemiah 8:10

"A merry heart maketh a cheerful countenance..."
Proverbs 15:13

"...A merry heart doeth good [like] a medicine."
>> Proverbs 17:22

"...But be of good cheer; I have overcome the world."
>> John 16:33

"Rejoice in the Lord alway: [and] again I say, Rejoice."
>> Philippians 4:4

"But let all those that put their trust in thee rejoice: let them ever shout for joy, because thou defendest them: let them also that love thy name be joyful in thee."
>> Psalm 5:11

29

Steps to Get There

Over the years I developed a self-reliant attitude due to interaction with the abusers in my past. My self-effort to gain victory in the area of eating only produced frustration. I learned over time to release the care of the eating disorder to God and trust the grace of God to help me.

As I understand it, grace is God's unearned, unmerited favor (**Ephesians 2:8**). The Bible says God has given to every man <u>the</u> measure of faith (**Romans 12:3**). Faith grows when it is fed the Word of God daily (**Romans 10:17**) and Jesus is the author and finisher of faith (**Hebrews 12:2**). Believers should rely on faith everyday in all areas of life (**Romans 1:17**). Faith along with patience (remain the same, steady), produce results (**Hebrews 6:12**).

The Bible says grace is given to believers (**Ephesians 4:7**) as a gift (**Ephesians 3:7**). Grace is available to anyone that will receive it (**I Peter 5:5**) and He is the God of all grace (**I Peter 5:10**). When I released the eating disorder to the grace of God, I felt like a weight was off my shoulders and was able to eat everyday.

"...My grace is sufficient for thee: for my strength is made perfect in weakness..."
II Corinthians 12:9

"And now, brethren, I commend you to God, and to the word of his grace, which is able to build you up, and to give you an inheritance among all them which are sanctified."

Acts 20:32

Everyday I seek God's wisdom in every area of life to grow spiritually (**Ephesians 4:15**). I want to increase in faith (**II Thessalonians 1:3**), knowledge (**Colossians 1:10**), favor and grace (**II Peter 3:18**).

Nourish the Whole Being

The body must be nurtured and cared for and not just from exercise and eating. The Bible says God created mankind as a three part being. The spirit, soul (mind, will, emotions) and body are interconnected (**I Corinthians 12:14**).

"And the very God of peace sanctify you wholly; and [I pray God] your whole spirit and soul and body be preserved blameless unto the coming of our Lord Jesus Christ."
I Thessalonians 5:23

Spending time "with myself" and speaking to my body encourages eating. When I talk to myself in a rough unloving tone I have very difficult days. My days are good when I speak lovingly, anoint or massage myself while speaking the Word of God. My body feels well and I am able to think about food and eat. I thank God for this revelation. Enjoying the time in my skin and walking by faith every day allow me to receive all God has for me.

"For no man ever yet hated his own flesh; but nourisheth and cherisheth it, even as the Lord the church."
Ephesians 5:29

"...His divine power hath given us all things that [pertain] to life and godliness."
II Peter 1:3

Today, I am blessed to have hunger pains. But when I ignore them, the desire to eat decreases for several days. When I feel hunger pains and respond by eating, the desire increases as well as the ability to eat a variety of foods.

Let me be clear, being aware of my body does not mean I am led or controlled by it. My spirit leads and guides my soul and body.

Expectation of Good

Today, instead of a sin conscious mindset I have a righteous mindset. The Bible says born again believers are "The righteousness of God by faith in Jesus" (**Romans 5:19**); "righteousness is revealed from faith to faith" (**Romans 1:17**).

"No matter how many times you have failed, how many mistakes you have made...Jesus Christ, is greater...our part is to believe in His goodness and wholeheartedly receive the abundance of grace and gift of righteousness from Him to reign victoriously over every area of defeat in our lives."
(Joseph Prince, www.josephprince.org).

"...Much more they which receive abundance of grace and the gift of righteousness shall reign in life by one, Jesus Christ."
Romans 5:17

"For the law of the Spirit of life in Christ Jesus hath made me free from the law of sin and death."
Romans 8:2

"...The worshippers once purged should have had no more conscience of sins."
Hebrews 10:2

"Holding faith, and a good conscience..."
I Timothy 1:19

Don't Give Up!

God hears and answers prayers that are in agreement with His Word. The Holy Spirit and heavenly angels work to bring His word to pass. Angels respond to the voice of God's word. That's my voice speaking His Word Praise God!

"And this is the confidence that we have in him, that, if we ask any thing according to his will, he heareth us:" "And if we know that he hear us, whatsoever we ask, we know that we have the petitions that we desired of him."
I John 5:14-15

"Bless the LORD ye his angels, that excel in strength, that do his commandments hearkening unto the voice of his word. Bless ye the LORD, all [ye] his hosts; [ye] ministers of his, that do his pleasure."
Psalm 103:20-21

"And ye shall eat in plenty, and be satisfied, and praise the name of the LORD your God, that hath dealt wondrously with you..."
Joel 2:26

Morning

Matthew 6:11
"Give us this day our daily bread."

Psalm 143:8
"Cause me to hear thy lovingkindness in the morning; for in thee do I trust: cause me to know the way wherein I should walk; for I lift up my soul unto thee."

Psalm 63:1
"O GOD, thou [art] my God; early will I seek thee: my soul thirsteth for thee, my flesh longeth for thee…"

Psalm 5:3
"My voice shalt thou hear in the morning, O LORD; in the morning will I direct [my prayer] unto thee, and will look up."

Isaiah 33:16
"…Bread shall be given him…"

Acts 16:34
"And when he had brought them into his house, he set meat before them, and rejoiced, believing in God with all his house."

Deuteronomy 12:7
"And there ye shall eat before the LORD your God, and ye shall rejoice in all that ye put your hand unto, ye and your households, wherein the LORD thy God hath blessed thee."

Praise

Psalm 107:1
"O GIVE thanks unto the LORD, for [he is] good: for his mercy [endureth] for ever."

Psalm 139:14
"I will praise thee; for I am fearfully [and] wonderfully made…"

Philippians 4:4-6
"Rejoice in the Lord alway: [and] again I say, Rejoice. Be careful (anxious) for nothing; but in every thing by prayer and supplication with thanksgiving let your requests be made known unto God. And the peace of God, which passeth all understanding, shall keep your hearts and minds through Christ Jesus."

Psalm 92:1
"IT [is a] good [thing] to give thanks unto the LORD, and to sing praises unto thy name…"

Deuteronomy 8:10
"When thou hast eaten and art full, then thou shalt bless the LORD thy God for the good land which he hath given thee."

Acts 14:17
"… Filling our hearts with food and gladness."

I Chronicles 29:22
"And did eat and drink before the LORD on that day with great gladness…"

Choose to Eat

Ecclesiastes 2:24-25
"[There is] nothing better for a man, [than] that he should eat and drink, and [that] he should make his soul enjoy good in his labour. This also I saw, that it [was] from the hand of God." "For who can eat, or who else can hasten (have enjoyment) [hereunto], more than I?"

Ecclesiastes 5:18
"Behold [that] which I have seen: [it is] good and comely [for one] to eat and to drink, and to enjoy the good of all his labour that he taketh under the sun all the days of his life, which God giveth him: for it [is] his portion."

Ecclesiastes 5:19
"Every man also to whom God hath given riches and wealth, and hath given him power to eat thereof, and to take his portion, and to rejoice in his labour; this [is] the gift of God."

Acts 9:19
"And when he had received meat (food) he was strengthened…"

Psalm 81:10
"I [am] the LORD thy God…open thy mouth wide, and I will fill it."

Acts 27:34
"Wherefore I pray you to take [some] meat: for this is for your health…"

Variety of Foods

Romans 14:2
"For one believeth that he may eat all things..."

Romans 14:14
"I know, and am persuaded by the Lord Jesus, that [there is] nothing unclean of itself: but to him that esteemeth any thing to be unclean, to him [it is] unclean."

Job 36:16
"Even so would he have removed thee out of the strait [into] a broad place, where [there is] no straitness; and that which should be set on thy table [should be] full of fatness (abundance)."

Psalm 81:10
"I [am] the LORD thy God...open thy mouth wide, and I will fill it."

I Timothy 4:3
"...Meats (foods), which God hath created to be received with thanksgiving of them which believe and know the truth."

I Timothy 4:4-5
"For every creature of God [is] good, and nothing to be refused, if it be received with thanksgiving: For it is sanctified by the word of God and prayer."

Meal Time

I Timothy 4:3-5
"...Meats (foods) which God hath created to be received with thanksgiving of them which believe and know the truth. For every creature of God is good, and nothing to be refused, if it be received with thanksgiving: For it is sanctified by the word of God and prayer."

Romans 12:2
"...Be ye transformed by the renewing of your mind, that ye may prove what is that good, and acceptable, and perfect, will of God.

Ephesians 4:23
"And be renewed in the spirit of your mind."

I Timothy 6:17
"...Who giveth us richly all things to enjoy."

II Peter 1:3
"According as his divine power hath given unto us all things that [pertain] unto life and godliness..."

Genesis 2:9
"And out of the ground made the LORD God to grow every tree that is pleasant to sight, and good for food..."

Romans 14:5
"...Let every man be fully persuaded in his own mind."

Healthy Eating

I Corinthians 10:23
"All things are lawful for me, but all things are not expedient: all things are lawful for me, but all things edify not."

Proverbs 19:8
"He that getteth wisdom loveth his own soul: he that keepeth understanding shall find good."

Proverbs 4:7
"Wisdom [is] the principal thing; [therefore] get wisdom: and with all thy getting get understanding."

John 21:13
"Jesus then cometh, and taketh bread, and giveth them and fish likewise."

Ephesians 5:17
"Wherefore be ye not unwise, but understanding what the will of the Lord [is]."

Psalm 32:8
"I will instruct thee and teach thee in the way which thou shalt go: I will guide thee with mine eye."

John 14:26
"But the Comforter, [which is] the Holy Ghost, whom the Father will send in my name, he shall teach you all things, and bring all things to your remembrance, whatsoever I have said unto you."

Joy in Eating

Proverbs 15:15
"...He that is of a merry heart [hath] a continual feast."

Ecclesiastes 9:7
"Go thy way, eat thy bread with joy..."

Ecclesiastes 8:15
"Then I commended mirth, because a man hath no better thing under the sun, then to eat, and to drink, and to be merry: for that shall abide with him of his labour the days of his life, which God giveth him under the sun."

Ecclesiastes 5:18
"Behold [that] which I have seen: [it is] good and comely [for one] to eat and to drink, and to enjoy the good of all his labour that he taketh under the sun all the days of his life, which God giveth him: for it [is] his portion."

Acts 27:36
"Then were they all of good cheer, and they also took [some] meat (food)."

Isaiah 55:2
"Wherefore do ye spend money for [that which is] not bread? and your labour for [that which] satisfieth not? hearken diligently unto me, and eat ye [that which is] good, and let your soul delight itself in fatness (abundance)."

Salvation Scriptures

"Therefore if any man [be] in Christ, [he is] a new creature: old things are passed away; behold, all things are become new."
II Corinthians 5:17

"And all things [are] of God, who hath reconciled us to himself by Jesus Christ..." II Corinthians 5:18

"...God was in Christ, reconciling the world unto himself, not imputing their trespasses unto them; and hath committed unto us the word of reconciliation." II Corinthians 5:19

"...We pray [you] in Christ's stead, be ye reconciled to God." II Corinthians 5:20

"For he hath made him [to be] sin for us, who knew no sin; that we might be made the righteousness of God in him." II Corinthians 5:21

"And it shall come to pass, [that] whosoever shall call on the name of the Lord shall be saved." Acts 2:21

"But the righteousness which is of faith speaketh..." Romans 10:6

"But what saith it? The word is nigh thee, [even] in thy mouth, and in thy heart: that is, the word of faith, which we preach;" Romans 10:8

"That if thou shalt confess with thy mouth the Lord Jesus, and shalt believe in thine heart that God hath raised him from the dead, thou shalt be saved." Romans 10:9

"For with the heart man believeth unto righteousness; and with the mouth confession is made unto salvation." Romans 10:10

"For whosoever shall call upon the name of the Lord shall be saved." Romans 10:13

"Then Peter said unto them, Repent, and be baptized every one of you in the name of Jesus Christ for the remission of sins, and ye shall receive the gift of the Holy Ghost." Acts 2:38

"How God anointed Jesus of Nazareth with the Holy Ghost and with power: who went about doing good, and healing all that were oppressed of the devil; for God was with him." Acts 10:38

"Howbeit when he, the Spirit of truth, is come, he will guide you into all truth...and he will [shew] you things to come." John 16:13

Made in the USA
Middletown, DE
16 June 2024

55548262R00035